First things first: My name is NOT Baby Bear. It's Sam. And I am not nearly as wee or small or tiny as people think.

And Goldilocks? Ever since she broke into my house, she's been one of my best buddies. It's true that she takes a lot of chances. But she's not a bad kid—at least, no worse than me. Let me tell you the REAL story, and you'll see.

ME

GOLDIE

WITHDRAWN

3

It all started when I complained about my breakfast. "Porridge AGAIN?" I said.

The next thing I knew, we were all out the door for a walk. Dad (also known as Papa Bear) grumbled something like, "He'll eat it if he's hungry enough."

At first I lagged behind.

"Stay where we can see you, Baby Bear!" called Mom (a.k.a. Mama Bear).

I ran ahead.

"Not so fast, Baby Bear!" called Dad.

I stamped my foot. "My NAME is SAM!" Then I ducked into the woods and took my secret shortcut home.

When I reached our house, I heard a voice. Someone was inside!

I didn't know what to do. Should I run to Mom and Dad for help? Or should I chase off the intruder myself?

BABY BEAR would have made a run for it. But not Sam.

I peeked through the kitchen window. A girl was taking pictures with her cell phone!

"Ha! This will teach Little Red Riding Hood to double-dare me," she muttered. "Goldilocks does not lose at Truth or Dare!"

She paused in front of the porridge bowls. "Eeeeeww," she said.

I liked her already.

Goldilocks took a picture of herself in my dad's chair ...

... then my mom's chair.

"You want proof, Little Miss Hoodie?" she asked. "Here it is!"

Next she took a picture of herself in my chair. When she got up, the chair stuck to her rear. She waddled around. She jumped up and down. Finally she gave the chair a good whack, and it came off—in pieces.

"Oops," she said. "There goes my allowance."

See? She meant to pay us back. Not that I cared—that chair was way too small for me too.

Upstairs, Goldilocks slipped off her shoes (which was very thoughtful of her) and took some video of herself jumping on my dad's bed. And my mom's bed.

"I can't believe I'm doing this!" she giggled.

Now, jumping on the beds is NOT ALLOWED in my house. This was my one and only chance to get away with it. I tapped at the window.

"ACK!"

Goldilocks shrieked.

"Let me in!" I begged. "I won't tell!"

Goldilocks opened the window, and we introduced ourselves. She apologized for breaking in. We were really quite civilized.

Then we **jumped** and **jumped** and **jumped** and **jumped** ...

... until we heard my mom calling from the woods. "Ba-by Bearrrr, where arrrre you?"

Goldilocks raised an eyebrow. "Baby Bear?" she asked. "Seriously?"

"Never mind!" I said. "Here's my plan …"

I ran downstairs just as my parents were coming in.

"Baby Bear!" Mom exclaimed. "Thank goodness you're OK."

"There's an intruder upstairs!" I said.

"You know better than to go around making up stories," Dad said.

They sat down to eat their porridge—their cold, dried-out porridge.

I brought in my broken chair. "See? The intruder did this!"

"What a naughty thing to do!" Dad said. "Wrecking a perfectly good chair just to get our attention."

"But I SAW her!" I insisted. "Come on!"

I tugged them upstairs and showed them the messy covers on their beds.

"Baby Bear, you know that jumping on the beds is a big no-no!" Mom scolded.

"But the intruder—" I said, pushing them toward my room.

And as soon as we reached my bed ...

"BOO!"

Goldilocks yelled.

What happened next was priceless.

"Run!" Dad cried.

"To our safe place!" Mom screeched.
"And if we don't make it—I love you both with all my heart!"

I made sure they saw me chasing
Goldilocks through the woods. In between
her fake screams and my pretend growls,
we traded phone numbers.

Mom and Dad were so impressed with my courage that they gave me everything I asked for: a bigger chair, spicy breakfast burritos instead of porridge, and a promise to stop calling me Baby Bear.

Well, there was one thing I didn't get.

"Can't I jump on the beds? Just once in a while?" I asked.

"NO," my parents said. "ABSOLUTELY NOT."

Hey, it was worth a try.

Think About It

Read a classic version of *Goldilocks and the Three Bears* and compare it to Sam's version. What are some things that happen in this story that don't happen in the classic? What are some things that happen in the classic story that don't appear in this one?

Most versions of *Goldilocks and the Three Bears* are told from an invisible narrator's point of view. But this version is told from Baby Bear's point of view. Which point of view do you think is more true? Why?

How do you think this story would be different if it was told from another character's point of view? What if Mama Bear told the story? Papa Bear? Goldilocks?

Sam doesn't think that Goldilocks was a bad kid, even though she broke into his house. Do you agree or disagree? Why?

What do you think would have happened if Sam had run back to his parents instead of seeing what Goldilocks was up to?

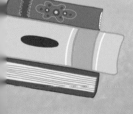

◦•◦❧◦•◦

Glossary

character—a person, animal, or creature in a story
narrator—a person who tells a story
point of view—a way of looking at something
version—an account of something from a certain point of view

Read More

Chichester Clark, Emma. *Goldilocks and the Three Bears*. Somerville, Mass.: Candlewick Press, 2010.

Child, Lauren. *Goldilocks and the Three Bears*. New York: Disney-Hyperion Books, 2009.

Guarnaccia, Steven. *Goldilocks and the Three Bears: A Tale Moderne*. New York: Abrams, 2000.

Spirin, Gennady. *Goldilocks and the Three Bears*. Tarrytown, N.Y.: Marshall Cavendish Children, 2009.

Internet Sites

FactHound offers a safe, fun way to find Internet sites related to this book. All of the sites on FactHound have been researched by our staff.

Here's all you do:

Visit *www.facthound.com*

Type in this code: 9781404866720

Look for all the books in the series:

Believe Me, Goldilocks Rocks!
Honestly, Red Riding Hood Was Rotten!
Seriously, Cinderella Is SO Annoying!
Trust Me, Jack's Beanstalk Stinks!

Super-cool stuff!

Check out projects, games and lots more at
www.capstonekids.com